COME HOME OFFICIAL WORKBOOK

PROPHETIC PRAYERS AND POWERFUL DECREES TO CALL YOUR PRODIGAL CHILD BACK TO GOD

TIM SHEETS

RACHEL SHAFER

CONTENTS

INTRODUCTION TO "COME HOME"

"Come Home" is more than a workbook; it's a transformative journey. This guide invites you to rediscover and deepen your Christian faith, reconnecting you with God's word and empowering your spiritual growth. Each chapter weaves together themes of redemption, transformation, and divine intervention, fostering a closer relationship with God and a deeper understanding of His presence in your life. Structured around key concepts, this workbook offers insights, reflections, and practical steps for personal growth and spiritual connection. It's a comprehensive guide, providing an immersive experience into significant spiritual themes.

* * *

Rediscovery of Faith: Central to "Come Home" is the idea of returning to faith, reminiscent of the prodigal son's journey in the Bible. This motif underscores the belief that a path back to spiritual fulfillment and connection with God is always available, no matter how distant one may feel.

Transformational Encounters: The workbook explores life-altering spiritual encounters, akin to the experience of Saul of Tarsus. These stories highlight the power of transformative moments to redirect life towards God's purpose.

Role of the Holy Spirit: A consistent theme is the Holy Spirit's guidance in personal transformation. You'll gain insight into how the Holy Spirit works within us, prompting a deeper contemplation of your spiritual journey.

Divine Intervention and Remembrance: "Come Home" emphasizes God's active intervention and fulfillment of His promises. It encourages recognition and appreciation of God's unfolding plan in your life.

Spiritual Awakening in Society: The workbook discusses the broader impact of individual spiritual awakenings. It shows how personal journeys of faith can influence and transform community values.

Community and Intercession: The importance of community involvement and intercession in spiritual movements is a recurring theme. You're encouraged to participate in your faith community and support others in their spiritual paths.

What to Expect

Deepened Understanding: Each chapter aims to enhance your grasp of Christian values, enabling you to integrate these principles into everyday life more effectively.

Personal Reflection: Through reflective questions and journal prompts, you're encouraged to introspect and connect personally with the content, deepening your exploration of your faith.

Actionable Steps: The workbook outlines practical steps to engage with and apply the lessons learned, promoting growth in your spiritual life and relationship with God.

Community Connection: Highlighting the role of community in the Christian journey, you are urged to share experiences, learn from others, and grow together in faith.

Empowerment and Inspiration: "Come Home" seeks to empower and inspire you to embrace your faith anew, actively participate in God's work, and positively impact your community.

As you begin "Come Home," prepare to be challenged, inspired, and transformed. This workbook is about experiencing and growing in your faith. It's an invitation to reconnect with God, rediscover your spiritual foundation, and join a movement of Christian revival and transformation. Welcome to a journey that leads you home – to the loving embrace of God, where your heart and soul truly belong.

* * *

HOW TO USE THIS WORKBOOK

Maximizing the Benefits of "Come Home" Workbook

To fully immerse yourself in and derive the greatest benefit from "Coming Home," it is crucial to approach this workbook with a deliberate and open mindset. Here are ten pivotal guidelines designed to guide you in harnessing the full potential of this enriching resource:

Establish a Routine: Dedicate a consistent time slot for engaging with this workbook. Consistency is pivotal in fostering a profound understanding and connection with the spiritual themes. Whether it's a daily or weekly ritual, discover a rhythm that aligns with your lifestyle and adhere to it faithfully.

Create a Conducive Environment: Select a space conducive to focus and reflection, free from interruptions. Be it a tranquil corner, a snug retreat, or a serene park, your chosen environment can significantly amplify your engagement with the content.

Engage with the Key Points Summaries: Begin each chapter by acquainting yourself with its key points summary. This overview provides insight into the chapter's primary themes, aiding in comprehending the core messages and their relation to the workbook's overarching narrative.

Reflect Deeply on the Reflective Questions: These questions are crafted to stimulate deep thought and introspection. Allocate ample time to ponder these, recording your reflections and emotions. This exercise is not about arriving at right or wrong answers, but about delving into your beliefs and experiences.

Implement Actionable Steps: Every chapter presents actionable steps, practical in nature, intended for incorporation into your everyday life. Experiment with these actions and observe their impact on your spiritual journey. True change often manifests beyond the confines of your comfort zone.

Use the Journaling Prompts: Journaling serves as a potent medium for personal evolution and self-exploration. Employ the provided prompts to delve into your thoughts, feelings, and reactions to the workbook's content. Journaling can unveil insightful revelations and is integral to the learning process.

Embrace the Words of Encouragement: Each chapter includes uplifting words of encouragement. Read these thoughtfully and reflect on how they resonate with your life and circumstances. They are meant to inspire and fortify your spirit.

Meditate on the Bible Verses: The selected Bible verses are fundamental to each chapter's theme. Dedicate time to meditate on these verses, comprehending their context, and pondering their relevance to your existence.

Discuss with Others: If feasible, engage in discussions about the workbook with friends, family, or a study group. Exchanging insights and experiences can deepen your understanding and offer diverse perspectives on the material.

Reflect on Your Progress: Periodically review your journey through this workbook. Contemplate how your perceptions and feelings have evolved. Acknowledging your development can be a powerful motivator and affirmation.

Additional Tips

- **Be Open to Change:** The workbook may challenge some of your pre-existing notions. Embrace these challenges as they present opportunities for growth and deeper comprehension.

- **Take Notes:** Feel free to annotate, highlight passages, or jot down notes. These personal annotations are invaluable in tracking your thoughts and epiphanies.
- **Pray for Insight:** Consider starting each session with a prayer for insight and openness. This can set a contemplative tone for your study and reflection time.
- **Revisit Chapters:** Do not hesitate to return to chapters that particularly resonate with you. Further readings can offer new insights or reinforce key concepts.
- **Balance Study and Practice:** While intellectual engagement with the workbook is crucial, it's equally important to apply the learned lessons. This harmony of study and application is where true spiritual growth takes place.

This journey is about more than reading; it's about engaging, reflecting, and integrating the lessons into your life. Embrace this opportunity for spiritual growth and personal discovery.

1

RESTORING LOST PURPOSE

In our journey through life, we often face moments that challenge our sense of purpose and direction. It's easy to feel lost or disconnected from our intended path. However, it's crucial to remember that no matter the detours or setbacks, our journey always holds the potential for rediscovery and renewal.

Hebrews 6:17-19 (NKJV): "Thus God, determining to show more abundantly to the heirs of promise the immutability of His counsel, confirmed it by an oath, that by two immutable things, in which it is impossible for God to lie, we might have strong consolation, who have fled for refuge to lay hold of the hope set before us. This hope we have as an anchor of the soul, both sure and steadfast, and which enters the Presence behind the veil."

. . .

In our quest to understand and reclaim our purpose, we begin by exploring the **Prodigal Son** story. This well-known parable is more than just an ancient tale; it reflects our own experiences of straying from and returning to our core values and beliefs. The story showcases how, despite any mistakes or distances we may have put between ourselves and our values, there's always a way back to redemption and purpose. The father's unconditional love in this story mirrors God's grace, teaching us vital lessons in forgiveness and acceptance. This narrative shows us that no matter how far we stray, there is always a path back to our true selves and purpose.

The **cultural context** of the Prodigal Son's story brings out its deeper meanings. The father's action of running, which was culturally inappropriate at the time, highlights the extent of God's grace. It shows us that God's love breaks through societal norms to reach us in our times of need. This part of the story helps us see that God's love isn't limited by what we think is normal or acceptable; it's far more vast and inclusive.

A key aspect of this chapter is understanding **God's unchanging plan for us**. Like the unwavering love of the father for his son, God has a steadfast plan for each of us.

This idea encourages us to see our lives as part of a bigger story, one carefully crafted with a specific purpose in mind. It reassures us that, even when we make mistakes or lose our way, God's plan for us doesn't change. This gives us both direction and comfort as we navigate life's challenges.

We also learn about the **power of redemption and restoration** in our lives. Our past errors or detours don't have to define us. Just like the Prodigal Son, we can always find opportunities for redemption and realignment with our original purpose. This key point reassures us that there's always a chance for a fresh start and a return to the path God has set for us, regardless of our past.

Another important aspect of the story is the **impact of humility and repentance**. The son's return is marked by an inner change—a realization of his wrongs and a humble return to his father. This teaches us that admitting our mistakes and learning from them is crucial in our journey toward fulfilling our purpose.

The **importance of community in our journey** is also highlighted. The story contrasts the community's potential negative reaction with the father's loving acceptance. This shows us that our community can either support us or present challenges in our journey toward purpose. Understanding this helps us see the value of having a supportive community that shares our values and goals.

The Apostle Paul's insights on purpose deepen our understanding of our divine calling. Paul's concept of a 'holy calling' suggests that our purpose is determined even before we are born. This perspective encourages us to look beyond our immediate situations and understand how we fit into a larger, divine plan. It's an invitation to consider how our individual stories are part of a greater purpose.

The idea of a **predestined purpose** in our lives provides a sense of stability and direction. Knowing our lives are part of a divine plan helps us make decisions and choose paths with confidence. This understanding gives us a feeling of security and helps us stay focused, especially during tough times.

Practically applying these biblical truths is crucial. The Prodigal Son story and Paul's teachings are not just theories but practical guides for living a purpose-driven life. They help us make choices and act in ways that align with God's plan for us.

Finally, the chapter focuses on **God's promise of restoration and redemption**. This promise reassures us that, regardless of how far we've gone astray or how many mistakes we've made, there's always hope for a turnaround. It's a reminder that our journey is supported by God's unending love and guidance.

This chapter invites us into a transformative exploration, urging us to look deeper into the themes of purpose, redemption, and our role in God's larger story. The journey through this chapter isn't just about gaining knowledge; it's about experiencing personal growth and transformation.

Reflective Questions

1. **How does the story of the Prodigal Son mirror your own life experiences?** Consider moments in your life where you've felt distant from your values and how you returned to them.

2. **In what ways can understanding the cultural context of biblical stories enhance your interpretation of their lessons?** Reflect on how the cultural insights into the Prodigal Son story have deepened your understanding.

3. **How does the concept of God's unchanging plan impact your view of life's challenges and setbacks?** Think about times you've strayed from your path and how this

perspective might change your response to these moments.

4. **In what ways have you experienced or can you imagine experiencing redemption and restoration in your life?** Look at your past experiences or current challenges through the lens of potential for redemption.

5. **How important is community in your journey towards fulfilling your purpose?** Reflect on the role of your community in supporting or challenging your path to fulfilling your purpose.

Actionable Steps

Cultivate an Understanding of Biblical Context: Begin by researching the cultural and historical background of the biblical stories you read. This will deepen your understanding and application of these stories in your life.

Equip Yourself with Humility and Repentance: Regularly assess your actions and thoughts, acknowledging mistakes and learning from them. This practice will keep you aligned with your true purpose.

Engage in a Supportive Community: Actively seek and participate in a community that shares your values and supports your journey towards fulfilling your purpose.

Journaling Prompt

Reflect on a time when you felt like you had lost your way, similar to the Prodigal Son. Write about how you felt during this time and what actions or thoughts led you back to your path. Consider the role of forgiveness, both from others and yourself, in this journey. How does this experience shape your understanding of purpose and redemption?

* * *

* * *

_____

_____

_____

_____

_____

_____

_____

_____

_____

_____

_____

* * *

_____

_____

_____

_____

_____

_____

_____

_____

_____

_____

_____

2

ANGELS OF EVANGELISM

Stand firm in the assurance that in these times of spiritual awakening, your role is pivotal. Embrace your identity as a child of God, empowered to bring forth His kingdom on earth. Let your faith be the guiding light in this journey of spiritual renewal.

"And it shall come to pass in the last days, says God, That I will pour out of My Spirit on all flesh; Your sons and your daughters shall prophesy, Your young men shall see visions, Your old men shall dream dreams. And on My menservants and on My maidservants I will pour out My Spirit in those days; And they shall prophesy."
Acts 2:17-18 (NKJV)

In **Chapter 2: Angels of Evangelism**, we delve into the unfolding of **supernaturally accelerated divine purposes**. This era is marked by an influx of promises, visions, and prophecies, with a distinct call for us to engage through prayer, faith decrees, worship, and embracing our identity in Christ. The chapter resonates with the teachings of Romans 5:17, emphasizing our reign with Christ.

We encounter the profound message of the Holy Spirit about the **merger of Christ's spiritual Kingdom on earth with the Kingdom of heaven**. This merger heralds a new phase in spiritual awakening, revealing God's power and authority on Earth like never before. This concept is not only inspiring but also places a responsibility on us to be active participants in this spiritual convergence.

A central theme is **angelic assistance in reaching our prodigals**. This idea offers hope and assurance, portraying the return of those who have strayed from their faith with the help of angels.

The chapter asserts the belief that the Holy Spirit is bestowing an unprecedented level of power from heaven, describing it as an unparalleled awakening and reformation, with a significant role for angel armies.

Acts 2:17-18 supports this, reinforcing God's promise to pour out His Spirit on all. This scripture acts as a validation of the current times and our role in this global spiritual movement.

The text also addresses the challenges posed by societal shifts away from spiritual truths, asserting that **hell has been striving to halt this great outpouring**. It discusses various tactics used to influence younger generations with non-Christian ideologies. However, the chapter assures us of the Lord's power and promise, envisioning the rise of a powerful Ekklesia, backed by angel armies, to stand against negative societal influences and lead a change.

The concept of **Evangelism Angels and the Harvest** is explored to explain angels' roles in the spiritual harvest process. The harvesting is described in three phases: **Phase 1** focuses on the return of prodigals; **Phase 2** on new believers joining God's Kingdom; **Phase 3** on revitalizing the role of evangelists in modern Christianity.

The chapter then shifts to a hopeful outlook for current and future generations, portraying a time when our children will actively engage in realizing God's plans, undergoing complete transformations in their lives. It emphasizes that no prodigal is beyond redemption, and God's power is sufficient for their complete liberation.

Finally, the chapter urges believers to **boldly confront current societal and cultural challenges,** emphasizing the power of spoken declarations and the role of angels in this battle.

Reflective Questions

1. How can you actively participate in the merger of Christ's spiritual Kingdom with the Kingdom of heaven?
2. In what ways can you offer support to prodigals seeking to return to their faith?
3. Reflect on how the Holy Spirit's power has manifested in your life or community.
4. Consider the societal challenges that confront Christian values. How can you make a stand against them?
5. What role can you play in the harvesting process as described in the chapter?

Actionable Steps

Cultivate a deeper understanding of your role in God's divine plan, especially in the context of the current spiritual awakening.

Equip yourself with knowledge and faith to support and guide prodigals back to their spiritual path.

Engage actively in your community to confront and address societal challenges that are contrary to Christian teachings.

Journaling Prompt

Reflect on the role of angels in your spiritual journey. How do you perceive their influence in your life and in the lives of those around you? Journal your thoughts and experiences, seeking a deeper understanding of this divine interaction.

* * *

* * *

_____

_____

_____

_____

_____

_____

_____

_____

_____

_____

_____

* * *

_____

_____

_____

_____

_____

_____

_____

_____

_____

_____

_____

3
HOPE SINGS

In the midst of your struggles, remember that God's presence is a constant source of comfort. His mighty power and boundless love envelop you, providing strength and hope. He is your steadfast companion, walking alongside you every step of the way.

Isaiah 41:10 (NKJV): "Fear not, for I am with you; Be not dismayed, for I am your God. I will strengthen you, Yes, I will help you, I will uphold you with My righteous right hand."

Chapter 3, titled "Hope Sings," delves into the journey of faith when confronted with the heartache of a loved one straying from their path. It starts with a powerful personal narrative, laying the foundation for exploring faith, fear, hope, and love in the face of adversity.

A central theme is **The Power of Persistent Prayer**, highlighting prayer as a vital lifeline in maintaining faith during challenging times. It's shown as a source of strength and comfort, offering an anchor in the storm of uncertainty and pain.

The chapter then addresses **The Role of Emotional Honesty**. Recognizing and confronting the array of emotions that arise from a family member's loss of faith is critical for spiritual growth and maintaining a true relationship with God.

In discussing **Understanding and Embracing Biblical Hope**, the chapter underscores hope as a confident expectation of God's promises, a firm belief in the unseen. Biblical stories illustrate this hope, encouraging readers to cling to it in their lives.

The balance of **Navigating the Tension Between Love and Truth** is also examined. This involves maintaining a loving relationship with someone who has strayed from faith, without compromising personal beliefs, by expressing faith with compassion and respect.

Engaging in Spiritual Warfare for Your Family is another focus. The chapter provides practical advice on actively fighting against negative spiritual influences through prayer and faith to protect and reclaim familial bonds and faith.

The Importance of Community Support is highlighted, stressing the need for support from fellow believers to offer encouragement and understanding in lonely times.

The Transformative Power of God's Love reaffirms that God's love can change hearts and circumstances, even in the darkest times, encouraging readers to keep believing in this transformative power.

Practicing Patience and Perseverance is emphasized, teaching the importance of trusting in God's timing and remaining steadfast in faith during the waiting period for a prodigal's return.

The Importance of Scriptural Anchors is discussed, highlighting the role of scripture in providing comfort and strength in times of doubt and fear.

Lastly, the chapter talks about **Fostering an Attitude of Expectant Faith**, encouraging a shift from hoping for change to actively expecting God to move in miraculous ways, based on trust in His promises and abilities.

* * *

Reflective Questions

1. How has your experience with a family member's departure from faith affected your personal relationship with God?
2. In moments of doubt or fear, what specific scriptures have provided you with comfort and strength?
3. Reflect on a time when persistent prayer played a crucial role in your life. What did you learn from that experience?
4. How can you balance expressing your faith with love and respect towards someone who has differing beliefs?
5. What role has community support played in your journey with a loved one who has strayed from faith?

Actionable Steps

Cultivate Emotional Honesty: Acknowledge and process your emotions regarding your loved one's faith journey. This may involve journaling, prayer, or conversations with trusted friends or mentors.

Equip Yourself with Scriptural Knowledge: Regularly read and meditate on scriptures that reinforce hope and faith. This practice can anchor you during challenging times.

Engage in Supportive Community: Actively seek and participate in a community that provides understanding and encouragement. This could be a church group, online forum, or a support group for those with similar experiences.

Journaling Prompt

Reflect on the current state of your relationship with your loved one who has strayed from faith. How has this situation influenced your understanding of God's love and power? Write down your thoughts, feelings, and any scriptures that come to mind, considering how this experience is shaping your faith journey.

* * *

* * *

_____

_____

_____

_____

_____

_____

_____

_____

_____

_____

* * *

_____

_____

_____

_____

_____

_____

_____

_____

_____

_____

_____

4

I WILL SAVE YOUR CHILDREN

In moments of uncertainty and challenge, remember that you are never alone. You are held within the steadfast promise of God's enduring love and protection. This assurance is not just a fleeting sentiment; it's a cornerstone of faith, a beacon in the storm. As you navigate the complexities of life, let this truth be your anchor, offering peace and hope.

"But thus says the Lord: 'Even the captives of the mighty shall be taken away, And the prey of the terrible be delivered; For I will contend with him who contends with you, And I will save your children.'"
Isaiah 49:25 (NKJV)

Chapter 4 opens our eyes to a remarkable spiritual awakening sweeping across the globe. This awakening, termed as the **Accelerating Global Spiritual Awakening**, is a powerful movement, ripe with divine synergy and blessing. It encourages you to reflect on your spiritual journey and its intersection with this global movement. Think about how this awakening has impacted your faith and your community, bringing a sense of unity and shared purpose.

The chapter further explores the critical role of the **Holy Spirit in Guiding and Empowering Believers**. The presence of the Holy Spirit is not just a theory; it's a tangible reality for many. Consider your own experiences or those within your community where the Holy Spirit's guidance was evident. These moments are more than personal; they are part of a collective narrative of divine interaction.

Another significant theme is the **Significance of Prophesy and Music in Revival Movements**. The chapter draws parallels with the Jesus Movement, where spiritual music played a pivotal role. Reflect on the role of music and prophesy in your faith. How have these elements influenced your spiritual life and helped spread hope?

The concept of **Simultaneity of Former and Latter Rains** presents a profound metaphor for spiritual growth. This imagery of simultaneous rains symbolizes an abundant spiritual outpouring. Reflect on how this metaphor relates to your spiritual growth and the current spiritual climate.

The chapter also emphasizes **Isaiah's Promise of Safety and Salvation for Children**. In a world fraught with cultural and ideological challenges, this promise is especially poignant. Think about how this promise is relevant today, especially in protecting and guiding the younger generation.

Prayer's power is central to the theme of **Role of Prayer and Intercession in Spiritual Awakening**. The chapter underlines the necessity of prayer in sustaining and advancing global spiritual movements. Reflect on your prayer life and its alignment with this global movement. How can you deepen your commitment to intercession?

Moving forward, the chapter highlights the **Impact of Spiritual Revival on Community and Society**. This revival is not just about personal experiences; it affects communities and societies at large. Reflect on the changes in your community and society due to this spiritual awakening.

Personal change is key, as discussed in the **Importance of Personal Transformation in Revival**. This section invites you to consider how your personal growth contributes to the larger movement. Think about the impact of your spiritual transformation on the broader revival.

The chapter also prepares us for **Anticipating and Preparing for Future Movements of the Holy Spirit.** As believers, we are encouraged to be ready for what comes next. Reflect on how you and your community are preparing for future divine movements.

Lastly, the **Role of the Church and Believers in the Current Revival** is examined. This part stresses the importance of active participation by the church and individuals in the spiritual awakening. Reflect on how you and your church can contribute to and engage in this movement.

Reflective Questions

1. How has the global spiritual awakening influenced your personal faith journey?
2. In what ways have you experienced or observed the Holy Spirit's guidance in your life or community?
3. Reflect on the role of music and prophesy in your spiritual life. How have these elements shaped your faith?

4. How does the metaphor of simultaneous rains speak to your spiritual growth and the current spiritual climate?

5. Consider the promise of safety and salvation for children in today's context. How is this relevant to your community and the world?

Actionable Steps

Cultivate a deeper understanding of the global spiritual awakening and its implications for your faith.

Equip yourself and others in your community with knowledge and resources that foster spiritual growth.

Engage actively in prayer and intercession, contributing to the collective spiritual awakening.

Journaling Prompt

Reflect on the intersection of your personal spiritual journey with the global spiritual awakening. Consider the role you can play in this movement, both personally and within your community. Write about your thoughts, feelings, and aspirations regarding your involvement in this global spiritual transformation.

* * *

I WILL SAVE YOUR CHILDREN

* * *

_____

_____

_____

_____

_____

_____

_____

_____

_____

_____

* * *

_____

_____

_____

_____

_____

_____

_____

_____

_____

_____

_____

5
COME HOME

In every step taken away from home, remember, the path to return remains open. Your journey back is not only possible but awaited with open arms. The story of the Prodigal Son is not just a tale of wandering but a celebration of return.

Luke 15:24 (NKJV)
"For this my son was dead and is alive again; he was lost and is found. And they began to be merry."

In **Chapter 5**, we go into the Prodigal Son's narrative, a story that resonates deeply with many. The journey of the prodigal is **The Universality of the Prodigal Experience**, reminding us that we may all, at some point, feel spiritually adrift, seeking our way back to a place of faith and belonging.

Central to this chapter is the concept of **The Father's Unconditional Love.** This profound love, which waits and watches for our return, no matter our past, is a testament to the boundless grace and compassion of the divine. This understanding is vital in appreciating God's readiness to welcome us back.

The Joy in Heaven Over One Sinner's Repentance illustrates the immense celebration that occurs in the spiritual realm when a person returns to faith. This joyous event is emphasized to show the significance of every individual's spiritual journey, valued both on Earth and in heaven.

The Role of Personal Conviction in Returning to God is highlighted, showcasing that like the prodigal son, our return is often driven by a deep personal conviction. This mirrors our spiritual awakening, often led by the Holy Spirit, guiding us back to our spiritual roots.

The Active Pursuit by the Father shows that, like the father in the parable, God actively seeks out His lost children, extending an open invitation for their return. This point underscores God's role in our spiritual journey and His relentless pursuit of our hearts.

Restoration and Celebration upon Return signifies the immediate restoration and joy that meets us upon our return, symbolizing God's eagerness to restore and rejoice over each soul that comes back.

The chapter also looks at **The Older Son's Perspective**, offering insight into feelings of jealousy and self-righteousness that can emerge within the faith community. This point serves as a caution against pride and the lack of compassion towards those returning from a period of wandering.

Addressing **The Church's Role in Embracing Returnees**, the chapter calls upon faith communities to welcome, forgive, and support those reintegrating into the faith, emphasizing the importance of a nurturing and accepting environment.

The Need for Continuous Prayer and Outreach is also emphasized, highlighting the communal responsibility in interceding for and reaching out to the lost or strayed, underlining our role as God's instruments in the world.

Lastly, **The Personal Call to Embrace Prodigals** invites believers to actively welcome back those who have strayed, encouraging them to embody the father's spirit in the parable through grace, love, and forgiveness.

* * *

Reflective Questions

1. How does the story of the Prodigal Son mirror your own spiritual journey? Reflect on times you've felt lost and how you found your way back.
2. In what ways can you relate to the father's unconditional love? Consider how this understanding of divine love has influenced your faith.
3. What emotions do you experience when reading about the older son's reaction? Explore your feelings towards those returning to faith after a period of wandering.
4. How can your faith community better support those who are returning? Think about the actions and attitudes that foster a welcoming environment.
5. What steps can you take to reach out to those who may feel lost? Identify practical ways to extend compassion and understanding to others.

Actionable Steps

Cultivate an Open Heart: Embrace those returning

to faith with an open heart and mind, reflecting the father's unconditional love in the Prodigal Son's story.

Equip Yourself with Understanding: Educate yourself and others about the importance of compassion and empathy for those who have wandered from their faith path.

Engage in Outreach: Actively participate in outreach efforts to reach those who feel lost, extending a hand of fellowship and guidance.

Journaling Prompt

Reflect on a time when you felt distant from your spiritual roots. What emotions did you experience, and what was the turning point that led you back? How can this experience inspire you to support others on their spiritual journey?

* * *

* * *

_____

_____

_____

_____

_____

_____

_____

_____

_____

_____

_____

_____

* * *

_____

_____

_____

_____

_____

_____

_____

_____

_____

_____

6

THE GOD HUG

God's embrace is a transformative experience, a manifestation of His unconditional love and acceptance. It's a reminder that no matter how far we stray, His arms are always open, ready to welcome us back with a love that changes everything.

"The Lord is merciful and gracious, slow to anger, and plenteous in mercy." - Psalm 103:8 (NKJV)

Chapter 6 takes us on a journey through the **parable of the prodigal son**, presenting it as more than a simple story. It's a profound reflection on God's love and forgiveness. This parable is not just about a son who strays, but a powerful demonstration of how eagerly God waits for our return, no matter our past mistakes. This story offers us a deep understanding of God's nature and how He relates to us.

One of the most impactful elements of this parable is the **depiction of God as a father who runs to meet his lost son.** This image is a departure from the common portrayal of God as distant and majestic. Instead, Jesus shows us a God overflowing with compassion, eager to restore our relationship with Him. It shows that God is not just watching from afar but is actively involved in our journey back to Him.

The chapter highlights the significance of the **'epipipto,' or the embrace of the Holy Spirit.** This Greek term from the parable symbolizes a loving, welcoming embrace. It encourages us to recall those moments when we've felt deeply loved, accepted, and forgiven by God. These experiences are crucial in our spiritual path, giving us a real sense of God's presence and love.

Furthermore, the story of **Peter and Cornelius** sheds light on the **inclusive nature of God's love.** This account from Acts illustrates how the early church realized that God's embrace was not limited to the Jewish community but extended to all, including Gentiles. This story is a powerful reminder that God's love is boundless and that the church's mission is to reflect this inclusivity, welcoming everyone regardless of their background.

Intercessory prayer is another key theme. The power of prayer, as shown through a mother's prayers for her son, underlines the influence our prayers can have. This serves as a reminder to persistently pray for those who have strayed, believing in God's power to transform their lives.

The concept of a **'God hug'**, a moment where we feel a deep spiritual connection and understanding of God's love, is central to this chapter. These moments can be life-changing, influencing our faith and perspective. They remind us of God's closeness and His readiness to accept us, no matter where we've been or what we've done.

The chapter also discusses the difference between **sonship and religious mindsets**. It compares the prodigal son's approach to seeking his father's love with the older brother's rigid adherence to rules, missing the essence of his father's love. This comparison challenges us to reflect on our own faith: Are we living in the joy of being God's children, or are we caught up in religious practices that prevent us from experiencing His love?

The **embrace of the Holy Spirit at Pentecost** and its effect on early Christians is a crucial point. This wasn't just a display of divine power, but an experience of God's love enveloping His people, reaffirming His acceptance and affection for them, irrespective of their past.

Transformation through God's embrace is also a central theme. The chapter illustrates how encounters with God's love can lead to significant changes in individuals and communities. This transformation goes beyond personal spiritual growth; it influences how we interact with the world, as we're motivated to share the love we've received.

Finally, the chapter emphasizes the importance of **ongoing renewal in the Holy Spirit**. Being a Christian is a continuous journey of being filled with God's love and presence. This constant renewal is vital for our spiritual well-being and our capacity to make a positive impact in the world.

In summary, Chapter 6 of "The God Hug" invites us to deepen our understanding of God's love and presence in our lives. It challenges us to see beyond traditional views of God, urging us to embrace a more personal and intimate relationship with Him, marked by continual growth and transformation.

* * *

Reflective Questions

1. **How have you experienced a 'God hug' in your life?** Reflect on moments where you've felt an overwhelming sense of God's love and presence.

2. **Consider the nature of God's love.** How does the image of God as a father eagerly running towards his lost child impact your view of Him?

3. **In your spiritual journey, have you ever felt like the prodigal son?** Explore times when you felt distant from God and how you were welcomed back.

4. **What role does intercessory prayer play in your life?** Think about how praying for others can influence their lives and your relationship with God.

5. **How can you better embrace God's inclusive love in your daily life?** Reflect on ways to extend God's love and grace to others around you, regardless of their background or beliefs.

* * *

Actionable Steps

Cultivate Regularly set aside time to meditate on God's love and presence in your life.

Equip Commit to praying for someone who may feel distant from God, believing in the transformative power of prayer.

Engage Seek opportunities to demonstrate God's inclusive love through acts of kindness and acceptance towards those different from you.

Journaling Prompt

Reflect on your own experiences of God's 'hug' – those moments where His love was unmistakably present. Write about how these experiences have shaped your faith and your understanding of God's love and grace.

* * *

* * *

_____

_____

_____

_____

_____

_____

_____

_____

_____

_____

_____

* * *

_____

_____

_____

_____

_____

_____

_____

_____

_____

_____

_____

7
CAST YOUR CARES

As you journey through this chapter, remember that you're not alone in your struggles. The worries that weigh you down are not yours to carry alone. Embrace the peace that comes from trusting in God's plan for you.

1 Peter 5:7 - "Cast all your anxiety on him because he cares for you."

In Chapter 7, we embark on a journey to understand the profound act of **casting our cares upon God**. The chapter begins with a touching story from an Oasis online member, illustrating the challenges and difficulties in family life and how these can be entrusted to God. This narrative sets the foundation for the entire chapter, illustrating the essential nature of placing our trust in God during times of stress and anxiety.

The chapter skillfully navigates the reader through the complexities of **recognizing the cycle of worry and trust**. It sheds light on a common struggle: even after we have prayed and given our worries to God, we often find ourselves taking these worries back, obsessing over them. This loop of worry and trust is a central theme of the chapter, depicted through personal stories and references to scripture, enhancing our understanding of the relationship between faith and worry.

A key focus of this chapter is the scriptural teaching found in **1 Peter 5:7**. The chapter breaks down this scripture to uncover its deeper meaning, emphasizing the action of 'casting' as a deliberate and strong gesture. This interpretation is crucial for understanding the level of commitment and decisiveness needed in letting go of our anxieties. The use of the Greek word 'epiripto' underscores the force with which we should 'throw away' our burdens, highlighting the intensity required in this act of faith.

The concept of **God carrying us through our trials** is another pivotal aspect of this chapter. Through a blend of personal experiences and biblical references, the chapter offers a comforting and reassuring message. The idea that God has been carrying us since our birth serves as a powerful reminder of His constant support and love, providing solace to those burdened by life's challenges.

Additionally, the chapter discusses the importance of **taking back what the enemy has stolen.** The story of David in 1 Samuel is used as an example, where David, against all odds, seeks God's guidance and ultimately recovers what he lost. This story is not just about victory; it underscores the power of faith and the necessity of being proactive in our spiritual battles, inspiring readers to reclaim their faith and trust in God's promise of restoration.

The power of **prayer and continual communication with God** is also a central theme of this chapter. Prayer is depicted as more than a religious practice; it is seen as an essential connection to the divine. This continuous dialogue with God is portrayed as crucial in casting our cares and maintaining our faith, as illustrated through various scriptural examples and personal stories.

Reminding ourselves of God's truth during difficult times is another important aspect the chapter explores. It encourages readers to focus on God's promises and His word, rather than giving in to fear and doubt. This shift from worry to the Word is essential in developing a mindset that finds strength and comfort in the promises of God.

The chapter also addresses the mental aspect of anxiety, emphasizing the importance of **taking every thought captive**. It highlights our ability to control our thoughts, aligning them with God's word to overcome fear and worry. Practical advice is provided to help readers combat negative thoughts and replace them with faith and scripture, making this a crucial part of the chapter's guidance.

A significant message in the chapter is **God's loving care and meticulous attention** to our lives. This message reassures readers that no part of their life is too minor for God's attention. Such understanding deepens trust in God's plan and timing, especially when the future seems uncertain or challenging.

Finally, the chapter concludes with an uplifting message on **expecting more than recovery**. Referencing the story of Job, it illustrates that God doesn't just restore what we have lost, but often blesses us even more abundantly. This message of hope and abundance is a powerful reminder of God's boundless grace and the rewards of unwavering faith.

* * *

Reflective Questions

1. **In what areas of your life do you find it hardest to cast your cares upon God?** Reflect on why these particular areas are more challenging for you.

2. **How can you identify and break the cycle of worry and trust in your life?** Think about the patterns that lead you back into worry and how you might disrupt them.

3. **When have you felt God carrying you through a trial?** Recall specific instances where you felt God's presence and support during tough times.

4. **What steps can you take to reclaim what you feel has been lost or stolen in your life?** Consider how you can actively seek God's guidance in these areas.

5. **How can you incorporate more prayer and scripture into your daily routine?** Identify practical ways to enhance your spiritual practice.

Actionable Steps

Cultivate Dedicate time each day for prayer, focusing on casting your cares onto God and seeking His guidance.

Equip Memorize key scriptures that reinforce God's promises and care, such as 1 Peter 5:7, to remind yourself of His presence in times of worry.

Engage Keep a journal to track your thoughts, worries, and the moments you feel God's presence. This can help in identifying patterns and moments of divine intervention.

Journaling Prompt

Reflect on a recent situation where you felt overwhelmed by worry or anxiety. Write about how you dealt with these feelings and how you might apply the lessons from this chapter to handle similar situations in the future. Consider the role of faith, prayer, and scripture in your response to anxiety.

* * *

* * *

_____

_____

_____

_____

_____

_____

_____

_____

_____

_____

_____

* * *

_____

_____

_____

_____

_____

_____

_____

_____

_____

_____

_____

8

I AM REMEMBERING YOU

In your moments of doubt and uncertainty, remember that God's presence is a constant source of strength. He is always there to guide and uplift you, even in the most challenging times. Trust in His unfailing love and let it be the beacon that guides you through life's storms.

"And the Lord, He is the One who goes before you. He will be with you, He will not leave you nor forsake you; do not fear nor be dismayed." - Deuteronomy 31:8 (NKJV)

In **Chapter 8 I Am Remembering You**, the narrative begins with a powerful **dream of prodigals returning**, portraying a widespread spiritual awakening. Picture a multitude, once estranged from their faith, now traversing diverse landscapes to reconnect with their spiritual roots. This dream signifies a significant and real return to Christian values and faith, affecting individuals across the globe.

The journey into the lives of **well-known individuals transforming** their lives, akin to Saul of Tarsus in the Bible, reveals people previously aligned with secular or anti-Christian values undergoing radical transformations. Their changes signify more than mere adjustments; they represent complete life overhauls, indicating a powerful and extensive return to faith and Christian values.

A pivotal element of this chapter is the **role of the Holy Spirit in guiding and enlightening** these individuals. The spiritual experiences they undergo are life-altering, prompting them to reevaluate their beliefs and life paths, similar to Saul's profound encounter, which drastically changed his life direction.

An important aspect is the **influential spheres these prodigals carry** in society. Their return to faith is not just a personal triumph but a beacon of societal change. Holding influential positions, they are capable of initiating significant shifts in societal values, moving from advocates of secular ideologies to champions of Christian values, signaling a larger movement of spiritual revival.

The author describes visions of **supernatural encounters** believed to be divine interventions crucial to the prodigals' journeys. These encounters are pivotal in pushing them to reevaluate their life choices and beliefs, emphasizing the belief in an active, interventionist divine force.

Central to this chapter is the concept of **'God remembering His people'**. It's about God actively intervening in human affairs, underpinning the events and transformations described. It reminds us that divine guidance is always present, even if not immediately apparent.

The chapter connects the **impact of divine remembrance on historical and present events**, illustrating the timeless and ongoing nature of divine intervention and suggesting a continuous divine involvement in human history.

Another crucial aspect is the **importance of recognizing and responding to divine signals** in life. It focuses on being aware of God's guidance, particularly in challenging spiritual times, urging readers to seek and recognize divine guidance.

The chapter also discusses the **transformative impact on families and communities**. The return of prodigals affects entire communities, highlighting how individual spiritual awakenings can lead to broader societal change.

Lastly, the chapter emphasizes the **role of intercessors and believers in nurturing this spiritual movement**, calling readers to actively participate in this process of spiritual renewal, aligning with the message of active faith and community involvement in the unfolding spiritual narrative.

Reflective Questions

1. **How has your personal journey mirrored the return of the prodigals described in this chapter?** Reflect on moments in your life where you felt a strong pull towards faith or a significant spiritual awakening.

2. **In what ways have you experienced or witnessed transformations in others similar to those described?** Think about the changes you've seen in yourself or others, especially those who have made a significant turn towards faith.

3. **How do you interpret the role of the Holy Spirit in guiding and enlightening individuals?** Consider your understanding of spiritual guidance and how you've seen it manifest in your life or the lives of others.

4. **What is the significance of 'God remembering His people' in your life?** Contemplate how this concept has played out in your experiences and how you've felt God's presence and action.

5. **How can you actively participate in nurturing the spiritual movement described in this chapter?** Think about ways you can contribute to a broader spiritual awakening, whether in your community or in your personal life.

Actionable Steps

Cultivate an awareness of spiritual transformation in your life and in your surroundings. Be mindful of the changes happening within you and around you that reflect a deeper connection to faith.

Equip yourself with knowledge and understanding of the Scriptures and Christian teachings. This will help you better recognize and appreciate the work of the Holy Spirit in your life and the lives of others.

Engage actively in your faith community. Participate in church activities, join prayer groups, or volunteer for community service. These actions not only strengthen your faith but also help spread the message of Christian love and compassion.

Journaling Prompt

Reflect on a time when you felt a deep connection to your faith, akin to the prodigals' return. Write about this experience, how it changed you, and what it taught you about God's presence in your life. Consider how this moment has shaped your spiritual journey and continues to influence your faith today.

* * *

* * *

_____

_____

_____

_____

_____

_____

_____

_____

_____

_____

I AM REMEMBERING YOU

* * *

FAITH AND FLAME PRESS

IGNITING THE FLAMES OF FAITH

Faith and Flame Press is a Christian book publishing company that is passionate about igniting the flames of faith in the hearts of readers around the world. Our mission is to publish books that inspire, enlighten, and uplift the spirit, and help readers deepen their understanding of their faith and spirituality.

At Faith and Flame Press, we believe that books have the power to transform lives and to shape the world we live in. That's why we are committed to publishing books that are not only spiritually uplifting but also intellectually stimulating, well-researched, and thought-provoking.